Betty Gibson

JUST DESIGNS

Just Designs focuses on the fun factor of creative embroidery. It is filled with exciting concepts in mixed media. The ideas illustrated are intended to fire the imagination and encourage the needlecrafter to be innovative with embroidery techniques combining ribbon and paint work.

Just Designs contains many designs for the reader to interpret in whatever colour, technique or thread seizes the imagination. These pages also contain some designs with labels, suggestions for stitches, colours and thread types. Some designs have a complete "how to" which will enable the less experienced needlecrafter to follow a design. The 100 plus colour plates show what has been achieved by others, thus encouraging the reader to produce works of creative merit.

Front cover: *A CELEBRATION OF EMBROIDERED FLOWERS.*
A tribute to Monet – (DI THOMPSON)
Paint, ink, ribbon and floss.

Back cover: *FIGURES IN THE FIELD* (TRIENIE KRUGEL) (Studio – Susan Sittig)
Overdye embellished with ribbon and floss.

Front page: *MONOGRAM WREATH* (ANAT GOLAN)

ISBN: 0-958 3873-6-2 … Hard Cover edition
ISBN: 0-958 3873-7-0 … Soft Cover edition

First Published 1996

PUBLISHED BY:
Triple T Publishing c.c.
29 Colenso Road
Claremont 7700
Cape Town, South Africa

NORTH AMERICAN DISTRIBUTOR
Quilters Resources inc.
P.O. Box 148850
Chacago II, 60614

Typesetting & Repro: Fotoplate, Cape Town
Printed by: Mills Litho, Cape Town

Text and photographs: Lesley Turpin-Delport.
Sketches: Lindy Gaisford and Lesley Turpin-Delport

Other books published by Triple T Publishing

SATIN & SILK RIBBON EMBROIDERY
by Lesley Turpin-Delport ISBN 0-620-17755-1

TWO CUSHIONS AND A QUILT
by Sue Akerman ISBN 0-958-3873-1-1

JUST FLOWERS
by Lesley Turpin-Delport ISBN-0-958-3873-3-8

THE LIBERATED CANVAS
by Penny Cornell ISBN 0-958-3873-4-6

© 1993 MANSELL PROMOTIONS LTD.,

Contents

Dedicated to
Sally Tarpey and Barbara Hughes

Authors Acknowledgements

My special thanks to all the needlecrafters who have contributed to this book:

Sue Akerman
Sandra Caister
Elaine Cohen
Nikki Delport
Rosemary Diamond
Nanda Dos Santos
Ann Foulner
Cynthia Friedman
Sharon Frittelli
Lindy Gaisford
Anat Golan
Kathy Hurwitz

Helen Jakoby
Shelly Jones
Trienie Krugel
Val Lane
Peggy La Trobe
Brenda Levine
Lesley Lewis
Sylvia Lewitton
Ali Marus
Sandy Meyer
Dean and Anne Neill
Ros Osrin

Gill Pilcher
Bridget Price
Evadne Quinn
Heather Roach
Clo Schaffer
Susan Sittig
Beryl Soller
Di Thompson
Lorna Van Staaten
Avril Walsh
Ethel Walt
Madge Wulfsohn

Sources of inspiration

Jemima Puddleduck - Beatrix Potter
Baby's Diary - Illustrated by Henriette Willebeek Le Mair
Edited by Dawn and Peter Cope
Inspiration for The Big Blue - Posters by John-Martin Jensen

Flower Fairies - Cicely Mary Barker
Greeting Card - by Noel Tatt and illustrated by Prue True
Calender - Newman Art Calender 1983
A Tribute to Great Artists - Claude Monet and Henri Matisse

Introduction

Just Designs is a culmination of many years of teaching and working with creative threads and fibre. Over a period of time, the constant request has been for "more drawings, please" "Where do you get ideas from?" has been the other query. In this book, I hope to share ideas, sources of inspiration, exciting techniques and a host of sketches for the reader to enjoy.

One of our greatest sources of inspiration is beautiful books. Buy gorgeous books – gardening books, children's story books, art books. Acknowledge your source of inspiration and grow from the genius of these wonderful authors and illustrators.

I have included some designs with labels, with suggestions for stitches, colours and thread type but obviously these can be treated in many different ways. The other designs are there for the reader to interpret, in whichever technique, colour and thread grabs the imagination.

"Just Designs" would not have been possible without the golden hands of my creative friends and teachers. The germ of an idea, grows from an interaction of inspired minds and dialogue and before you know it, fibre and thread work together and the magic carpet ride begins.

Lesley Turpin-Delport

ROCKING CHAIR (NIKKI DELPORT.)

SMOCKED ANEMONES AND SEA URCHINS

This detail from *MARINE TREASURE TROVE*, page 42 illustrates the amazing dimensions possible if the creative imagination combines different techniques and textures. Here hand-painted silk has been smocked, pulled up into circles and embellished with beads and embroidery stitches. Gauze and crepe bandage has been coloured with vibrant silk paint and worked into exciting shapes using colonial knots and extended french knots. The background silk has great depth, achieved by using salt crystals on the fabric while the silk paint is still wet. The crystals absorb the paint and leave exciting amoebic shapes behind.

THE RIGHT NOTIONS

A box of crayons, pots of paint, threads, cottons and silks create embroidery notions. When you feel like a little fancy work, select exciting fabric and choose the right needle and thread to match, these are part of the little pleasures of life that give so much enjoyment.

Embroidery is a creative process. Free your imagination and experiment with threads and express your creativity.

THREADS

Stranded Cotton (Floss)

A shiny six strand thread which can be split into 1, 2, to 6 threads according to the thickness of the fabric, the desired effect and the embroiderers special know-how. It is the best choice for cross stitch, padded and unpadded satin stitch and crewel embroidery.

Perlé Cotton

Shiny, twisted thread, ideal for beginners: it does not come untwisted and thus ensures uniform stitches. Excellent results on medium, coarse linen and Aïda fabrics.

Soft Cotton

(Tapestry cotton)

Thick, matt thread, 100% cotton is very easy to use on coarse or basket-weave canvases. Soft and flexible.

Coton A Broder/Flower Thread
Fine, matt cotton thread.

Tapestry Wool
Suitable for embroidery on softly textured, loosely woven material.

Crewel Wool
Mothproof, 100% pure virgin wool, soft and fine, ideal for delicate wool work.

Pure Silk, rayon, viscose, linen and metallic thread
These are a number of other thread types which are exciting when mixed together to create different textures and colour combinations. Some craft shops have hand-dyed, variegated threads which are marvellous for free style embroidery.

Quilting threads
Commercial quilting threads are now available in all colours, but if you can't find any, use a pure cotton thread (No 30) and run it through beeswax to prevent it tangling.

Ribbons
(Pure silk, raw silk and satin ribbon)
Pure silk ribbon is available in 2mm, 3.5mm, 7mm and 13mm. It is so soft that it can be pulled through the background fabric just like embroidery floss. Rayon ribbon works well using the silk ribbon techniques. Raw silk webbing can be manipulated onto the background fabric and pulled through, if the fabric is not too fine. Satin ribbon is best manipulated off the background fabric. Construct leaves and flowers as free-form shapes and then work them onto the background using invisible stitches.

EMBROIDERY SCISSORS
Light with fine, pointed ends to cut thread cleanly.

THIMBLE
A must for embroidery comfort.

Detail from the *WHEEL BARROW*. (See page 33 for a full picture. Page 57 shows colour sketch.) Terra-Cotta pots; silk, pen and paint.

VALENTINE ANGEL
(BRIDGET PRICE)
Inspired by wrapping paper.
Embroidery hoop, ribbons and floss.

EMBROIDERY FABRICS
All fabrics can be used for embroidery.
Embroidery fabrics which are highly recommended:
* fine and medium fabrics; pure linen, pure cotton, linen cotton mixture
* more open fabrics to make counting threads and stitches easier, such as coarse linen and even-weave. (Aïda 14 count).
* Exotic fabrics such as moiré taffetta, pure silk, raw silk, velvet, fine corduroy and antique handkerchiefs.

EMBROIDERY FRAME
The cloth, stretched on the frame, does not pucker. Various frames are available. They can be held in the hand, fixed to a stand or to the edge of a table, they come in several diameters.

NEEDLES
* Use crewel (embroidery) needles for fine embroidery. Sharp tip, small eye.
* Chenille needles for candlewicking and silk ribbon embroidery. Sharp tip, long eye.
* Tapestry needles for woollen embroidery. Blunt tip, long eye.
* Straw (or sharps) needles for specialist stitches such as bullion and cast-on buttonhole. Very small eye, long shaft.
* Between needles for quilting. Small eye, very short shaft.
* Bead needles for beading. Small eye, long and very thin shaft.

BEADS
A selection of tiny seed beads, pearls and bugle beads is very handy to work into your embroidery for shine and dimension.

PERMANENT MARKERS
A permanent black fine-liner is used in the mixed media designs. Always test your pen to see that it is in fact colour fast. Different nib widths are available for fine or coarse work. Ink in your outline before you begin the paintwork.

FABRIC PAINTS
A water based, permanent paint is ideal.

9

Try different size paint brushes: a fat stiff bristle brush will give a good stipple or drag effect; a medium size, stiff bristle brush is good for the smaller areas and a small fine brush is needed for delicate detail.

Begin by testing your paint on a small piece of scrap fabric to gain a little confidence. Use the paint, very diluted, to give the delicate water colour effect. Dry paint will give a good stipple and a creamy consistency is best for filling in. Heat seal the paintwork by ironing with a hot iron. The black outline can be worked into with a permanent fine marker if you have painted too darkly.

ANTIQUE VEIL (Courtesy of LORNA VAN STRAATEN)
Pure silk roses.

HEMLOCK, (AVRIL WALSH)
Silk ribbon and floss on damask.

CHERUB, (CYNTHIA FRIEDMAN)
Wire edged, organdie and silk ribbons.

FRIVOLOUS FUN

This chapter is dedicated to the needlecrafter who enjoys experimenting with fun techniques and ideas that can speed up the creative process.

FABRIC PAINTING

Painting your fabric speeds up the creative process and offers many different, exciting effects depending on the method you choose to colour your cloth.

There are many different fabric paints available. **Any** paint can be used if the cloth is not going to be washed.

I use permanent fabric paint, stencil paint, aerosol and silk paint on any natural fibre, if the art work must be permanent.

There are three principle mixtures for fabric paint;

1. Straight out of the bottle with a dry, stiff bristle brush for a stipple or drag effect.
2. The paint and a little water mixed to a creamy consistency for filling in and controlled paint work.
3. Very little pigment with a lot of water for a wash or water-colour effect.

Always allow the fabric to "peep" through here and there – this gives life and light to the background.

Silk paint on cotton fabric gives a terrific translucency and the colours are very vibrant. Wet the cotton fabric and apply the silk paint liberally over the surface. Allow the colours to run into each other and many different effects can be achieved. To achieve a really "fun" effect, sprinkle salt crystals on the wet surface, with the fabric laid out flat and in the sun. The salt absorbs some of the colour and when the fabric dries, wonderful images of effervescence, bubbles, anemones etc. are left behind on the fabric.

Aerosol paint sprayed onto the fabric gives a stippled effect which can be used for sky or grass. Do not hold the can too close to the fabric and do not apply the paint too thickly otherwise the needle will not penetrate the fabric easily when you embroider.

MARINE TREASURE TROVE (ROSEMARY DIAMOND)
Multiple choice and magpie abundance. All this and colour too.

PHOTOS TO FABRIC

The naked canvas or blank paper is always daunting to the prospective artist. An easy way to accomplish a professional finish is to colour your cloth with a photocopy transfer and then embroider the finer details.

MATERIALS REQUIRED

- Solvent – lacquer thinners • A soft rag • Cardboard
- A colour (or black/white) photocopy of photograph or illustration • Fine cotton or polycotton fabric • Masking tape • A soup spoon

---

METHOD

Make a colour photo copy of the picture you wish to transfer. Ask the photocopy technician to "bump up" the colour of your photocopy. (This will give a good colour transfer).
Work on a melamine surface or a piece of smooth cardboard. Position your fabric on this surface using masking tape to keep it in place. Now place the photocopy, face down, over the fabric. Hold the copy in position with a strip of masking tape on one side. Saturate the rag with thinners and using a firm, rotating motion work into the back of the photocopy. Now take the soup spoon and re-inforce the motion by "spooning" the toner from the photocopy into the fabric with the back of the spoon.
Check your progress by gently lifting the photocopy to see all the toner has, in fact, penetrated the fabric. Once you are happy with your transfer, iron the design from the back to heat-seal it. Accent the important areas with free-style embroidery.

TIPS FOR SUCCESSFUL PHOTO TRANSFERS

- Choose a clear picture with good contrasts.
- Do not overload your rag with thinners. This can cause the toner to bleed into the background fabric.
- Stay small. Too large a design is not a good idea.

GUINEA FOWL (SUE AKERMAN)
Create an ethnic flavour with a photo-transfer on chamois leather.

AUTUMN LEAVES, (SUE AKERMAN)
3D Applique embellished with metallic threads.

RIBBONS

The silk ribbon technique described on pages 49-54 can be used for any ribbon which is soft enough to pull through the background fabric. There are wonderful ribbons available if one starts to really look around – soft cotton ribbon, rayon ribbon, ribbon found in knitting shops usually only considered suitable for knitting and last but not least organdie ribbon. Organdie ribbon is superb for diffusing colours on colour photo-copies and for overlaying on silk ribbon . Organdie ribbon is best handled in stab stitch and controlled and worked into with stranded cotton (embroidery floss). Good examples are illustrated in Trout (page 41) and African Butterflies (page 27).

WIRE EDGED TAFFETA RIBBON

Extravagant and truly frivolous fun can be had with ombre, wire edged ribbon. This ribbon is shaded in colour and has a thin copper wire running along each side of the ribbon. By pulling the copper wire on one side, the ribbon ruffles and can be manipulated to create the most beautiful old-fashioned roses. Begin by making a knot in the ribbon. Pull the wire, gather, roll and stitch the base of the ribbon as you create your rose. Once the rose is the required size, sear the raw edge of the ribbon by passing it along the base of a flame. Fold this end under and coil the copper wire around the base of the rose. Stitch the rose in place with a matching thread and then manipulate the petal shapes by bending the copper wire on the upper edge of the ribbon.

Rose leaves work well by forming a folded triangle and then bending and manipulating the shape to snuggle into the blooms. There are many different flowers you can create from wire edged ribbon. Have fun and experiment with the potential of this versatile medium.

METALLIC THREADS

Metallic threads give an exciting sheen and highlight to a design. Keep the thread short and if necessary, pass it through bees-wax for better control.

They are ideal for insects, butterflies and fairies.

ROSE POMANDOR (SHELLEY JONES)
(Studio – Lorna van Straaten)
Satin ribbon cabbage roses.

RED BERET (CLO SCHAFFER)
In silk ribbon.

HEART BOX (SHELLEY JONES)
(Studio – Lorna van Straaten)
Satin ribbon roses, pearls and
cherub charm.

JEWELLERY BOX
(DI THOMPSON)
Decorated with
wire-edged
pansies.

14

BEST FRIENDS

This chapter pays tribute to the wonderful talent of children's story book writers and illustrators, who fire the imagination and allow the child in us to live forever. BEATRIX POTTER, CICELY MARY BARKER, PRUE TRUE, HENRIETTE WILLEBEEK LE MAIR were the source of inspiration for the embroidery on the following pages.

FROM DAVID WITH LOVE
(LES AND NIKKI DELPORT)

This delightful design is essentially crewel wool and perlé thread. The Source of inspiration is the inset photograph, and a complete "how to" is provided on page 64.

15

FOR RUPERT AND ABIGAIL
(DI THOMPSON)

A charming companion piece for the two little bears on
the previous page.
This design combines ribbon work, candlewicking,
trapunto quilting and some free style embroidery.
The source of inspiration was the photograph below.
A complete "how to" is provided on page 65.

TWO LITTLE MICE (PRUE TRUE) (Embroidery EVADNE QUINN)
Muslin ribbon overlaid with tiny colonial knots is a quick solution for strawberries, with flowers of white silk ribbon, using the 3D petal method described on page 54. The dress and apron are created in organdie ribbon, overlaid with multi-coloured colonial knots. The yoke and hem are frilled, using the ruched ribbon technique on page 54.

JEMIMA PUDDLE DUCK AND THE FOX (BEATRIX POTTER) (Embroidery GILL PILCHER)
The interpretation of these famous characters in silk ribbon and fine crewel work is quite delightful – Notice the woven waistcoat and stab-stitch pantaloons of the fox and trapunto overlaid with split stitch silk ribbon feathers of Jemima. The background is a symphony of stitches in perlé and stranded cotton.

17

DUTCH DELIGHTS

The delightful pictures on this page were inspired by the exquisite illustrations by HENRIETTE WILLEBEEK LE MAIR from *BABY'S DIARY*.

Notice the sensitive interpretations in silk and organdie ribbon. Fine details are in single strand crewel stitches with the heavier work in perlé cotton thread.

PEEK-A-BOO
(SANDY MEYER).

MOTHER AND CHILD
(SANDY MEYER).

HIDE AND SEEK. (SANDY MEYER).

DRY THE TEARS (BRENDA LEVINE).

LITTLE MICE

(Embroidery BERYL SOLLER).

(Inspired by a calendar)

Recreated with pen, paint and crewel stitches.

'UQUET BUNNY.

ACORNS GALORE.

HAPPY BIRTHDAY

SWING TIME

BIG BONNET.

FURRY FRIENDS.

IN DUET.

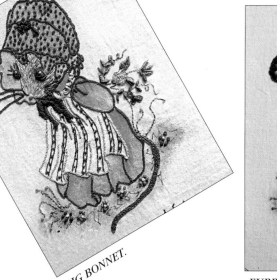

MOTHER & SON.

19

FAIRIES
(CICELY MARY BARKER)

Go out and buy the beautiful collection of *FLOWER FAIRY* books by Cicely Mary Barker – they provide mouth-watering inspiration for interpretation in ribbon and thread. In the examples shown, the uniqueness of the individual shines through. The fairy and flower provide the needlecrafter with a challenge to choose from a host of stitches, metallics and ribbons and then to create the sensitive balance between fantasy creature and flower.

THE SWEET-PEA FAIRY – (BRIDGET PRICE)
Ruched in ribbon in 3,5mm and 7mm gives a splendid dimension to the sweet-peas; complimented by fine stitchery in single strand floss.

THE LAVENDER FAIRY – (ALI MARUS)
Silk ribbon in mock bullion for the blooms and stab stitch for the skirt is a perfect choice here. Double-sided cast-on buttonhole leaves, lazy daisy waist-band and chain hair, are all stitches which can be found in the stitch glossary.

THE SLOE FAIRY – (GILL PILCHER)
The silk ribbon is ideal for a dress of inverted stab stitch. A wonderful interpretation of wings is achieved with colonial knots, buttonhole, overcast stem and stab stitch in floss and metallic thread. Different dimensions occur in the fruit with colonial knots of silk ribbon and floss while the leaves are fishbone, rumanian and picot.

THE WILLOW FAIRY – (CYNTHIA FRIEDMAN)
Muslin (or gauze) ribbon for the foliage and organdie ribbon for the delicate skirt – indeed an ideal choice for this particular fairy Fine stab stitch creates an illusion of water beneath the ethereal figure.

THE VEGETABLE PATCH

Vegetables – the life source of good health! If we cannot persuade our children to eat them, we can have fun designing and creating them in ribbon and thread.

LANDSCAPE VEGETABLE PATCH
(LES LEWIS AND LES DELPORT)

Ink in the basic outlines; add a light wash of fabric paint and enjoy ribbon and crewel embroidery in simple stitches as you create your different vegetables. (See the labelled sketch on page 66 and 67 overleaf for more details).

THE LANDSCAPE VEGETABLE PATCH

Below: Detail showing, *LETTUCE AND CAULIFLOWER*
Lettuce in various shades of ruched silk ribbon, make an exciting contrast with the crewel wool, cast-on buttonhole and perlé thread, colonial knot cauliflower.

Top right: Detail showing, *RUNNER BEANS*
Double-sided cast-on buttonhole makes an ideal choice of embroidery stitch for garden beans. By the way this stitch is also ideal for tiny worms.

Bottom right: Detail showing, *TOMATOES AND CORN ON THE COB*
Colonial knots in shades of tomatoe red are complimented by variegated green silk ribbon leaves in lazy daisy. The corn on the cob is a combination of colonial knots, picot and tufting.

THE FORMAL VEGETABLE PATCH (MADGE WULFSOHN)
Hedgerows, crazy paving, vegetables and herbs combine in r

Brinjal, strawberries, celery and kale.

Mushrooms, chives, brussel sprouts, lettuce and beetroot.

Dill, beans, radish and cauliflower.

Rhubarb, cabbage, carrots, broccoli, spring onions, sprouts.

bbon and crewel embroidery.

23

A BURST OF GOLDEN SUNFLOWERS
(LES LEWIS & LINDY GAISFORD)

Vibrant silk paint on cotton fabric creates the perfect foil for many different ribbons combination. The petals are simply stab stitch in various ribbon types with centres of colonial and bullion knots.

Below: SUNFLOWERS (ETTY SERY)
Variation on a Theme – Detail
A rich centre of seeds is achieved with colonial knots, cast-on buttonhole and tiny spider's web. Ripple quilting gives added texture to the surface.

LITTLE CREATURES

Without the marvellous creatures of this world our vegetable patches and secret gardens would cease to exist. These designs show some of the magical fun the reader can have playing with the pen, paint, ribbon, metallics and stranded cotton, designing realistic or fantasy creatures.

CREEPY CRAWLIES
(LESLEY TURPIN-DELPORT AND SANDRA CAISTER)

Colour your cloth with fabric paint, in gentle washes and enjoy the different interpretations of these little creatures. Notice what fun it is to experiment with organdie ribbon, metallic thread and single strand floss. Treat a few of the creepy crawlies in a bold manner, with a lot of ribbon and thread and handle others with a delicate touch of embroidery. A complete "how to" is provided on pages 70 and 71.

25

ETHEL'S BOX

Design a box of your favourite flowers and complimentary insects.

Right: In the design, a tiny bumble-bee, with silver buttonhole wings and bullion body, buzzes between the proteas, heather and grasses. The *proteas* are single strand bullions in the centre, in pale pink floss, changing to cast-on buttonhole, in light and rose pink floss. Try a straw needle for bullion and cast-on buttonhole. These stitches slide off the needle so easily if you use the right notions. The leaves and stems are overcast stem in grey-green and pinky-brown floss. The *heather* is made up of a series of bullions, beginning with six twists and increasing by two twists on either side; working from the centre outwards, in dark pink floss through to the palest shade of pink. The *hair-bells* are in pink single strand chain and the lilac grass is bullion and whipped backstitch.

Below: A dragonfly, with silver backstitch wings and statin stitch and bullion abdomen, hovers delicately over a branch of *erica*. The petals are overcast stem, bright pink at the tips changing to pale pink at the centre. The leaves are rumanian in two strands of avocado green. A friendly snail completes the picture. The shell is brown single strand buttonhole and the body is beige, single strand colonial knots.

Below right: The tiny ladybirds are single strand, satin stitch in red floss with black, colonial knot spots, stab stitch legs and feelers and white satin stitch head.

TINY BUMBLE-BEES on proteas, heather and grasses.

DRAGON-FLY AND SNAIL on Erica.

LADY-BIRDS on heather.

AFRICAN BUTTERFLIES
(LES TURPIN DELPORT)

Labelled sketch on page 74 and 75.

ORANGE AND LEMON (ERONIA LEDA).

ROTHSCHILD DILUTE GREEN
(CHARAXES DILUTUS).

CAMBRIDGE VAGRANT
(NEPHERONIA TALASSINA).

QUEEN PURPLE TIP (COLOTIS REGINA).

YELLOW AND BLUE PAIR (Butterflies).

CATERPILLARS.

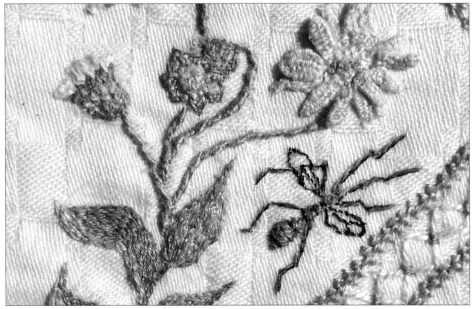

ANOTHER GNAT.

CREWEL & METALLIC THREAD BUTTERFLY.

SECRET GARDENS

Flowers, glorious flowers. A source of joy to the creative needlewoman. Photograph your secret garden and create your own beautiful work. The following pages will help to provide ideas.

A QUITE CORNER
(ANAT GOLAN)

Create a quiet corner of proteas, aloes, gypsophila, arums, irises, roses, sunflowers and all the other flowers you can think of, by combining silk ribbon and floss in crewel stitch mixtures. Allow pen and paint work to peep through the embroidery to achieve greater depth to the design.

THE GAZEBO
(LINDY GAISFORD AND LES LEWIS)
A fine sketech which lends itself to interpretation of silk ribbon flowers and crewel stitches. 3D Petal daisies, spiders web roses, and ruched ribbon creepers complete a delightful scene.

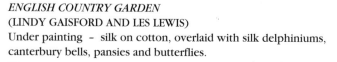

ENGLISH COUNTRY GARDEN
(LINDY GAISFORD AND LES LEWIS)
Under painting - silk on cotton, overlaid with silk delphiniums, canterbury bells, pansies and butterflies.

TWIN POTS.
(LINDY GAISFORD AND LES LEWIS)
Silk paint on cotton overlaid with ribbon embroidery. See page 56 for a colour sketch.

CARDS - *PANSIES* (NANDA DOS SANTOS).

CARDS - *LITTLE VIOLETS* (NANDA DOS SANTOS)
uick and easy way to create a special greeting card. The even-weave fabric
da 14 count) allows the needelcrafter the scope of manipulating the ribbon
controlling the tension to suit different petals. Simple stab stitch and
tonhole provide the finishing touches.

Source of Inspiration for,
DELPHINIUMS.

LARKSPUR AND DELPHINIUMS (HELEN JAKOBY)
Ink and underpainting provided the foundation for this textured piece of
work. Many different ribbons have been used to suite the scale of the
blooms; silk, rayon and muslin ribbons. The leaves are organdie ribbon
worked into position with fly stitch and feather stitch.

31

THERE IS A SEASON
(LINDY GAISFORD & ANNE NEILL)

Ink the basic design, add a little silk paint for a
background wash, and enjoy the crewel work.
Turn to pages 68 and 69 for the sketch and
complete instructions on "how to".

E WHEEL BARROW (LINDY GAISFORD AND SHARON FRITTELLI)
chelors buttons in buttonhole pinwheels, silk ribbon and floss daffodils and a multitude of
ferent daisies spill out of an old fashioned wheelbarrow. A different interpretation of these pots
l be found on page 8. Turn to page 57 for a colour sketch.

THE GREEN HOUSE (LINDY GAISFORD AND ANNE NEILL)
Ink sketch worked with ruched rayon ribbon, bias-cut orchids and Japanese silk violets.

SANDERSON STYLE
(BRIDGET PRICE)

Sanderson linen was the inspiration for this
cushion design of cabbage roses and single
strand silk embroidered bows.

FUN WITH FISH

The embroidery in this chapter is an interpretation of how marine animals and plants interact with one another. The idea behind the designs is to make the reader aware of our marine heritage and how fragile it is.

DETAIL FROM THE BIG BLUE

See page 37.

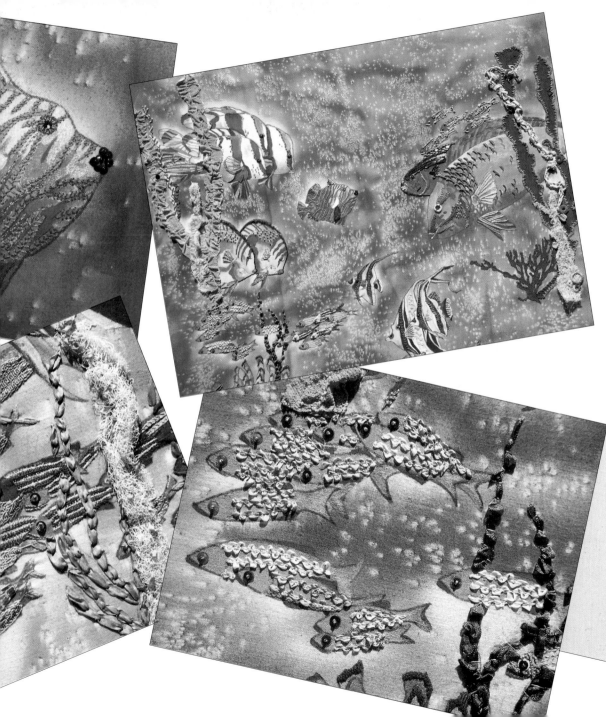

THE BIG BLUE
(ELAINE COHEN)

Immediate left: Silk and stencil paints, glitter paint and ribbon embroidery give the silvery illusion of scales to a shoal of fish.

Seed beads, sequins and bugle beads add opalescence. Stitch tiny beads onto the eyes for that extra "glitz". Sea-weed of loofah (rough sponge) and silk ribbon compliment the shoal of fish. Loofah is cut into strips, threaded with silk ribbon and stitched in place with ecru thread. The fish are high-lighted with silk ribbon and metallic feather stitch.

Crepe bandage sea-weed, painted with silk paint, is gathered up the centre and "scrunched" in place with chain stitch. The background bubbles are created by sprinkling salt crystals on cotton fabric saturated with silk paint.

Below: TURQUOISE DELIGHT (KATHY HURWITZ)
A sensitive use of metallic threads combined with traditional crewel stitches. Notice the fine control of bullions on the upper fin in single strand rayon thread.

37

MARINE LIFE

Below: *OCTOPUS, RAY, SHRIMP & SEAHORSE*
(KATHY HURWITZ)
Fabric appliqué overlaid with exciting stitches, such as raised chain and weaving, create new textures. Each of the marine images will be embellished to the full, the excess fabric cut away, leaving a small seam-allowance which is turned under and the design hand appliquéd to the background fabric.

Right, bottom: *CRAB* (KATHY HURWITZ)
A celebration of bullion and colonial knots.

Right, top: *THE GOLDFISH BOWL – A Tribute to Matisse*
(DEAN & ANNE NEILL)
Soft water-colours on cotton, with embroidered accents in many different crewel stitches.

AQUAMARINE on opposite page ▶
(LESLEY TURPIN-DELPORT & ANNE NEILL)

The following selection of unusual fabrics were used: Linen, snake skin, velvet, moiré taffeta, hessian and suede. These fabrics are combined with approximately fourteen different yarns, ranging from exotic wools, tapestry cotton, mercerised cotton, six strand floss, metallic thread to pure silk ribbon.

Texture and the third dimension is important in the design, as well as, the accuracy of the creatures being represented. Trapunto (Italian quilting) gives the nautilus shells, barnacles, periwinkles and starfish a special dimension. Tiny seed beads add sparkle which is complimentary to the metallic threads and a suggestion of motion is created by the delicate movement of ostrich feathers.

The entire design is hand embroidered except for the outlines of the fish forms which are machine appliqued. Strips of linen fabric are cut, then knitted and interwoven with raffia to form the rocks. Metal washers are covered with crewel wool and filled with french knots, bullions, and buttonhole bars to give the illusion of anemones. Silk ribbon embroidery makes an interesting contrast with the crewel wool interpretation of the plants. The stitches used are raised chain, feather stitch, wheatear, split stitch and coral stitch.

(A humerous note is provided by the cleaner shrimp STENOPUS HISPIDUS with its gaudy colours and transparent gut. Simple and composite stitches are combined to stimulate the potential embroiderer).

There is a deliberate contrast in scale between the large starfish and barnacles, in fabric, and the smaller version, in the lower zone, in embroidery thread only. Certain images are focal and bold while others require a discovery of the treasure trove beneath the waves.

MARINE CREATURES – OCTOPUS, RAY, SHRIMP, SEA HORSE (Work in progress).

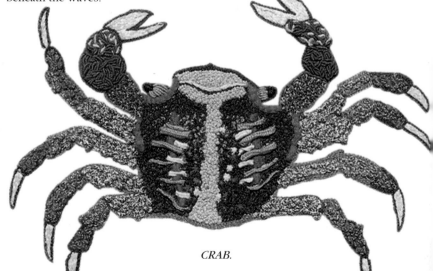

CRAB.

SALMON AND TROUT FLIES
(SANDY MEYER)

Create a grid of whipped chain on moiré taffeta and make a sampler of different salmon and trout flies. The "feathered" effect of the flies is achieved by positioning rayon and organdie ribbon under the overcast stem shaft. Once the bullion barbs are made and the metallic threads have been wrapped around the shaft, the protruding ribbons are then frayed by separating the warp from the weft with a straight pin. Other free-standing stitches such as detached picot, and turkey-work (tufting) are also used. For really fine bullions use a single strand of sewing machine thread. The interesting border is wrapped card-board. Cut a suitably coloured strip of mount board and wrap the ribbon around the board, securing it at the back with glue or a few tiny stitches.

FRESH WATER TROUT
(HEATHER ROACH)
Photo-transfer, overlaid with organdie ribbon
and embellished with metallic thread.

MARINE TREASURE TROVE
(ROSEMARY DIAMOND)

Right: Discover the treasures of different fabrics, textures, techniques and stitch combinations.

Bottom right: Detail showing, *SEA-HORSE, PORTUGUESE MAN-OF-WAR*
The sea-horse is gauze bandage, hand-painted and embroidered with cast-on buttonhole in variegated perlé threads.
The Man-of-war is organdie appliqué stuffed with polyester wadding and tendrils of different wools, string and perlé threads. Notice the raw-edged smocked tail of the fish on the lower right.

Middle: Detail showing, *BLUE CHENILLE OCTOPUS AND SMOCKED SEA URCHINS*
The sea urchins are smocked fabric, pulled up into a circule stuffed and embellished with bead details.

Bottom left: Detail showing, *SEA URCHINS AND ANEMONES*
Ruched circles, embellished with bullion, colonial knot and bead details.

SEA URCHINS AND ANEMONES.   BLUE CHENILLE OCTOPUS AND SMOCKED SEA URCHINS.   PORTUGUESE MAN-OF-WAR, SEA HORSE AND FISH.

IMPRESSIONS

Enjoy the different ideas and techniques illustrated in this chapter and interpret the sketches provided at the back of the book, bearing these fabulous concepts in mind.

ON THE TERRACE
A work in progress (ROS OSRIN)
Inspired by a Claude Monet's Terrace at Saint-Dresse.
Even a sporting event can be translated into exquisite embroidery. A deck view of a yacht race combines ribbon and crewel embroidery, worked into a light impression of watercoloures. Note the delightful wicker chair in weaving stitch and overcast stem. The tall pink Watsonias are stab stitch with a difference – two ribbons are threaded through the needle simultaneously and stabilised with a yellow colonial knot.

43

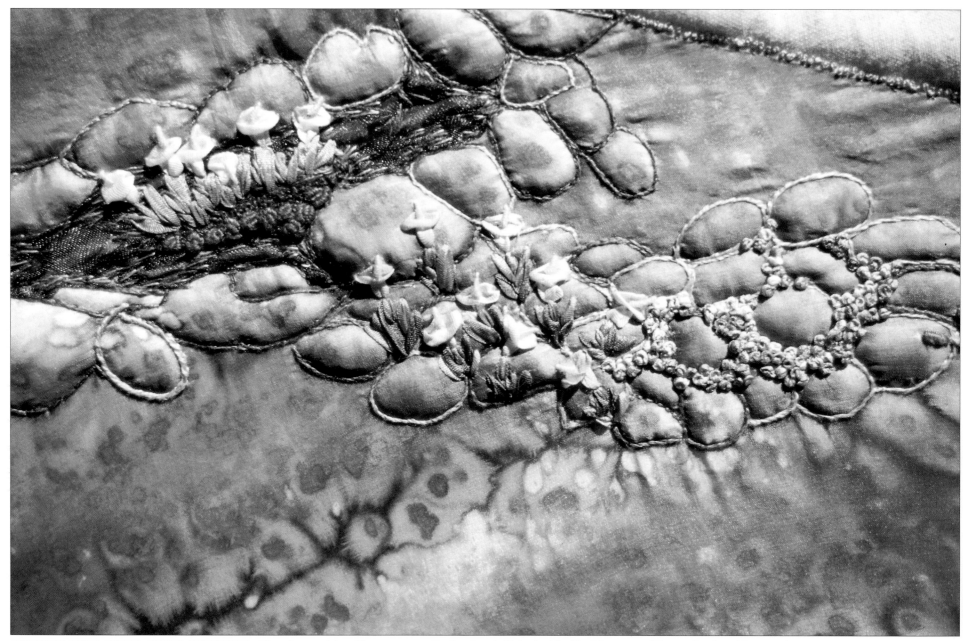

LILYPOND WITH ARUMS (SYLVIA LEWITTON) Silk paint on china silk, trapunto quilted and embellished with silk ribbon arum lillies and colonial knot rocks..

STRIPED ODALISQUE.

LADY WITH A VIOLIN.

NUDE ON ORIENTAL CARPET.

CREATE AN IMPRESSION

Embroider your own home! If you can paint, you don't have a problem, but if you can't here is an easy way to colour your cloth. Take a good photograph of your house and have a colour photo-copy made. Ask the technicians to enlarge if necessary and don't forget to tell them to reverse the design otherwise your house will face the wrong way! Now follow the instructions on page 12 in Frivolous Fun and *transfer* the image onto your fabric.

An alternate method of colouring your cloth: make a black and white photo-copy from a photograph of your home. Enlarge the design to suit. Place the enlargement behind your fabric, on a light box. Ink in the basic outlines with a permanent marker. Now have fun and follow the ideas on page 11 in Frivolous Fun on *painting* the fabric yourself. See picture below.

Once you have an impression of your house on fabric, draw inspiration from the houses illustrated here and select stitches to suit your own home and garden.

PEGGY LA TROBE'S HOUSE Ink and paint preparation.

46

Rambling roses on *VICTORIAN PORCH* (VAL LANE)
(Studio – Lorna van Straaten).

BARGEBOARD-HOUSE (ROS OSRIN).

VICTORIAN FILIGREE (ROS OSRIN).

WINDYBROW (ANN FOULNER).

RED-TILED ROOF (ROS OSRIN).

ON A CLEAR DAY (ANN FOULNER AND LINDY GAISFORD) Underpainting with fine crewel and silk ribbon details.

WORKING WITH RIBBON AND RIBBON STITCHES

FLORAL SAMPLER
(ANN FOULNER)

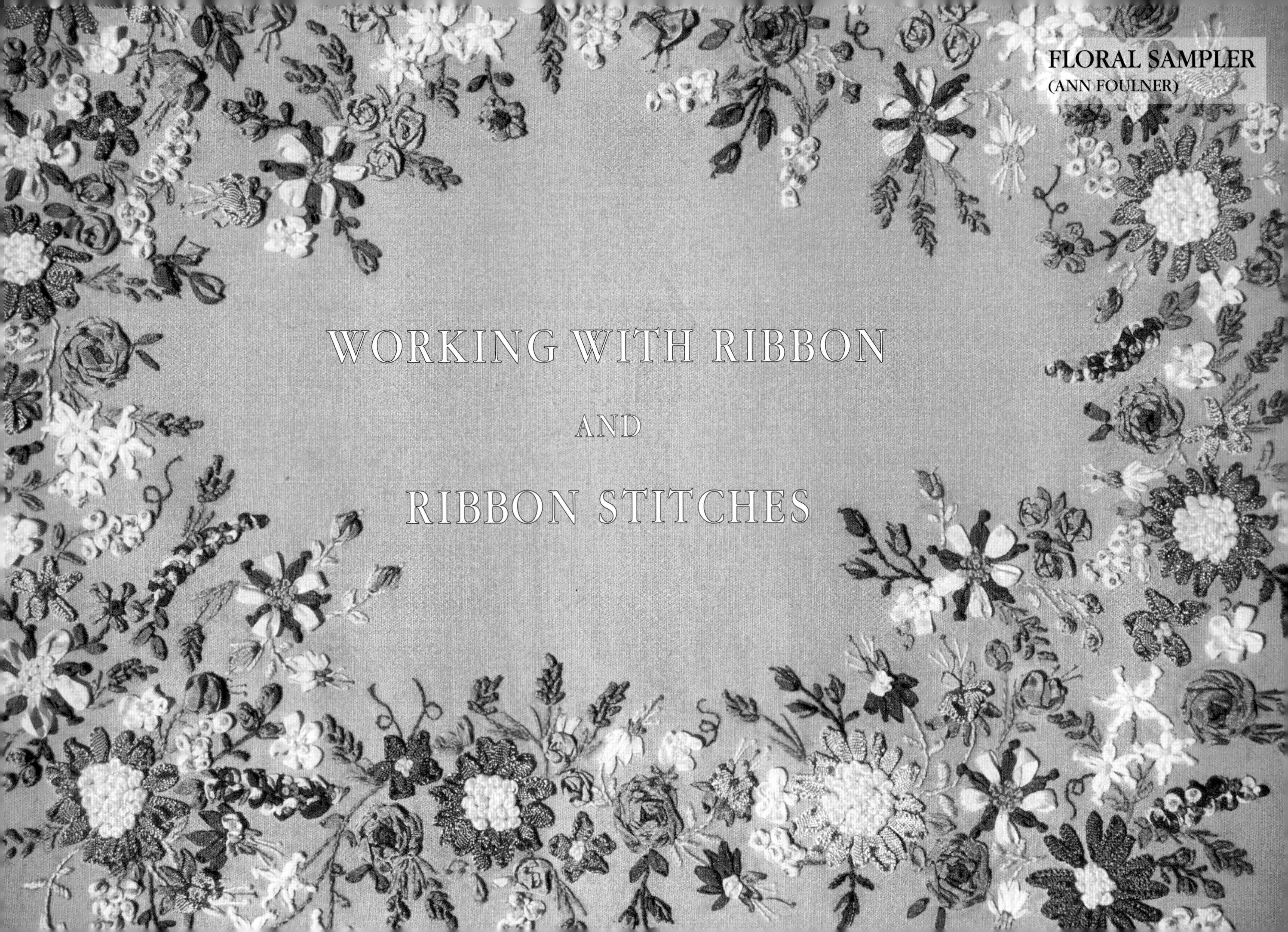

WORKING WITH RIBBON

These methods can be used for all types of ribbon eg. velvet, satin, rayon and taffeta ribbon.

MAKING RIBBON ROSES

THE CABBAGE ROSE (OR TAB METHOD)

(Using approximately 8-10mm ($^3/_8$-$^1/_2$″) wide satin ribbon)
Cut a short length of ribbon approx 6cm (2″). This is the tab.
Fold the tab over the end of the ribbon length, forming a square with the ribbon **(a)**.
Form the bud centre of the rose by rolling the ribbon tightly on itself, a few times, to make a tight tube. Make a couple of small stitches at the base to hold it firm **(b)**.
To form the petals, fold the ribbon backwards so that it is parallel to the tube, forming a 45 degree angle. Roll the tube across the fold, loosely at the top and tightly at the base. Stitch in place with a couple of stitches **(c)**.
Continue to fold, roll and stitch, shaping the rose as you work, until it is the desired size. Cut and sear the ribbon by quickly passing it under the base of a candle flame or lighter.
Turn the end under the rose simulating a petal and slip-hem in place. Cut off the excess tab and sear the base of the rose.
Once you have made a selection of roses, position them onto your background fabric and stitch them in place with tiny, invisible stitches.

RIBBON LEAVES

Using ribbons approximately 1.5cm ($^5/_8$″) wide, cut a rectangle of ribbon approx 8cm (3$^1/_4$″) in length. Sear the raw ends by passing the ribbon through the base of a flame.
Fold the top corners to the centre to form a mitred triangle. **(a)**
Run a gathering thread along the seared edges. Pull the gathers up firmly to form the leaf shape. **(b)**
Tuck this edge under the rose and stitch it firmly to the background. **(c)**
For a stronger leaf, use a double thread brought through the tip of the leaf and secure it into the background.

50

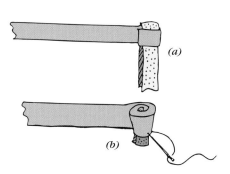

(a)

(b)

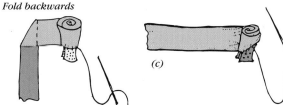

Fold backwards

(c)

Cut off excess tab

(a)

(b)

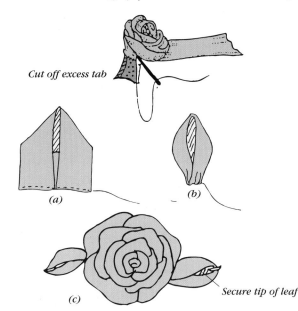

Secure tip of leaf

(c)

Satin ribbon roses.
(Cabbage rose.)

Tafffeta ribbon leaves with wire edged ribbon roses. See page 13.

Working with silk ribbon.
This example shows silk ribbon leaves with bias cut china silk flowers.

Trout with organdie ribbon overlay.

Keep the ribbon flat as it is threaded in and out of the fabric and control the tension on the ribbon and you will be thrilled with the result.

SILK AND ORGANDIE RIBBON

Embroidery with silk ribbon is fun and quick to do. The stitches used are the same as those used in traditional embroidery floss, but the silk ribbon gives the stitches exciting dimensions.

LENGTH OF RIBBON

Cut the ribbon, at an angle, approx 30cm (12″) in length. Too long a ribbon will fray and twist, which will not enhance your embroidery.

TO THREAD THE NEEDLE

Thread the ribbon through the eye of the needle, pull the ribbon through approx 2″ (5cm) and pierce the ribbon approx 1cm (½″) from the end. Pull the long end of the ribbon downwards until the ribbon locks into the eye of the needle. This prevents the needle from unthreading while you work.

HOW TO BEGIN

I like to work with a muslin foundation behind the background fabric. This is not always necessary but usually gives the work more body and also allows for a neat ending. Begin by leaving a small tail hanging at the back of your work. As you make your first stitch, pierce the tail with a needle to secure the ribbon.

Some needlewomen find the tail securing difficult while doing tricky combinations. If this is the case make a small backstitch in the muslin foundation. Do not jump from one part of the design to another, as the colour might show through the background fabric, and you might cause a pucker. To prevent puckering, you should work with a small 3″ (8cm) embroidery ring.

TO FINISH OFF YOUR STITCH

Take the ribbon through to the back and work a small backstitch into the muslin foundation and through the ribbon. Be careful not to snag the embroidered ribbon in that area OR leave a tail which can be caught in, when the next thread is started.

POPULAR STITCHES IN SILK RIBBON

STAB STITCH
These are single spaced stitches worked either in a regular or irregular manner. Sometimes the stitches are of varying size. The stitches should be neither too long nor too loose.

INVERTED STAB STITCH
Bring the needle through the background fabric and at the tip of the shape, pierce the ribbon and the fabric in the same movement. Pull the ribbon gently through forming a 'nipped' tip.

SPLIT STITCH
Make a single straight stitch. Now bring the needle up through the ribbon, piercing the centre of the stitch from below, dividing the ribbon exactly in the middle. Repeat, forming a neat line of stitches.

FLY STITCH
Make a satin stitch but come up in the centre of the stitch at a diagonal. Pull through and anchor the stitch with a small tying stitch.

COLONIAL KNOT
Pull the ribbon through the fabric. Place the needle under the ribbon, sliding the needle from left to right. **(1)**
Wrap the ribbon over the top of the needle from right to left creating a figure eight. **(2)**
Insert the needle into the fabric close to where it emerged; pull the working ribbon taut with your left hand so that a firm tight knot is formed. **(3)**
Pull the needle to the wrong side of the fabric forming a colonial knot. Come up at the next dot. **(4)**

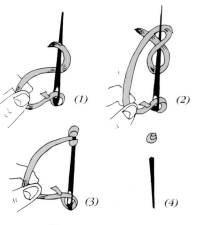

COLONIAL KNOT AND LAZY DAISY ROSEBUDS
The rosebud is a combination of a colonial knot surrounded by a lazy daisy.

Stab and inverted stab stitch.

Fly stitch.

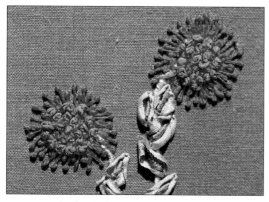

Stab stitch and bullion leaves.

Mock bullion and bullion lazy daisy.

Split stitch and bullion lazy daisy.

Irish stitch.

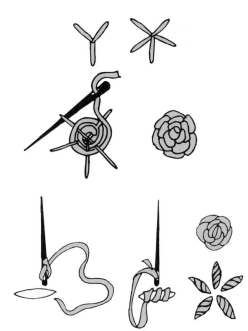

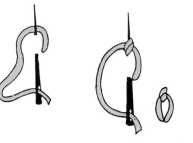

WOVEN SPIDER'S WEB ROSE

Make five foundation spokes in two strands of matching embroidery floss. Then use the silk ribbon and weave over and under each spoke, starting in the centre and working outwards, controlling the tension as you proceed. Once the spokes are covered and the rose is the required size, take the ribbon through to the back and end off with a backstitch in the foundation fabric.

MOCK BULLION

Make a stab stitch as your foundation. Use the back of the needle and wrap the ribbon around the stab stitch, three or four time, moving along the stitch. Turn around the top of the stitch and wrap the stab stitch three or four times again, moving down the stitch length.

BULLION-LAZY DAISY

Make a single chain stitch and before anchoring it, twist the ribbon twice around the tip of the needle. Pull the needle through the ribbon and anchor into the background.

IRIS STITCH

Make a single chain stitch and anchor it with a small straight stitch. Bring the ribbon through the fabric on the lower right of the chain. Using the back of the needle, slip the ribbon under the base of the chain loop.

Anchor the ribbon on the lower left of the chain stitch, re-entering the background at this point.

Make a yellow colonial knot or bullion in the centre of the chain stitch in two strands of floss.

53

WEAVING STITCH

This stitch is very effective if you want to create the illusion of a basket weave. Make a series of long stitches, side by side, the width of one ribbon apart. With a blunt needle and using a contrast ribbon, weave over and under the ribbons, starting at the widest part. Push the ribbons together as each line is worked so that even squares of each colour appear.

Weaving stitch.

LOOPED 3D PETAL (DAISIES)

Make the looped daisies last as they are rather fragile. Cut a 20cm (8″) length of ribbon for each daisy. Do not remove the pins until the base of each petal is secured with a colonial knot (or french knot) in two strands of yellow embroidery floss. The centre can be embellished with extra french knots or stamens in extended french knots.

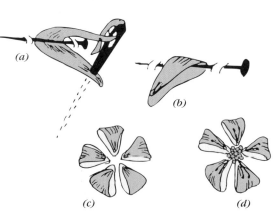

(a)

(b)

(c)   *(d)*

3D Petals.

RUCHED PETALS FOR FUCHSIAS, HIBISCUS, CARNATIONS AND MARIGOLDS

Bring the silk ribbon through the background fabric. Use a crewel needle with one strand of matching floss and run a gathering thread along one side of the ribbon. Pull up the gathers to create the fluted petals. End the gathering thread securely and pierce the background fabric with the silk ribbon, forming a gathered frill. End each frill with a backstitch on the wrong side of the work.

BASIC FUCHSIA

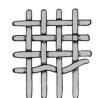

Pedicel

Calyx

Corolla
(Petals)

Stamen

Pistil

FUCHSIA WITH A DOUBLE WHORL OF PETALS

FLUTED/RUCHED PETALS

silk ribbon

gathering
thread

*Ideal for a double
whorl of petals*

Fuchsia.

COLOUR WASHES
AND
MONOTONE
SKETCHES

Use the sketches, to form the basis for your original embroidery – adapt them to suit your own ideas, enlarge them if need be – above all, enjoy them and have fun.

Where there is an embroidered version, the page number is marked.

JUST THATCH

TWIN POTS

(See page 30 for an
embroidered version
with silk ribbon
and floss.)

WHEELBARROW

(See page 33 for an embroidered version.)

FUCHSIAS

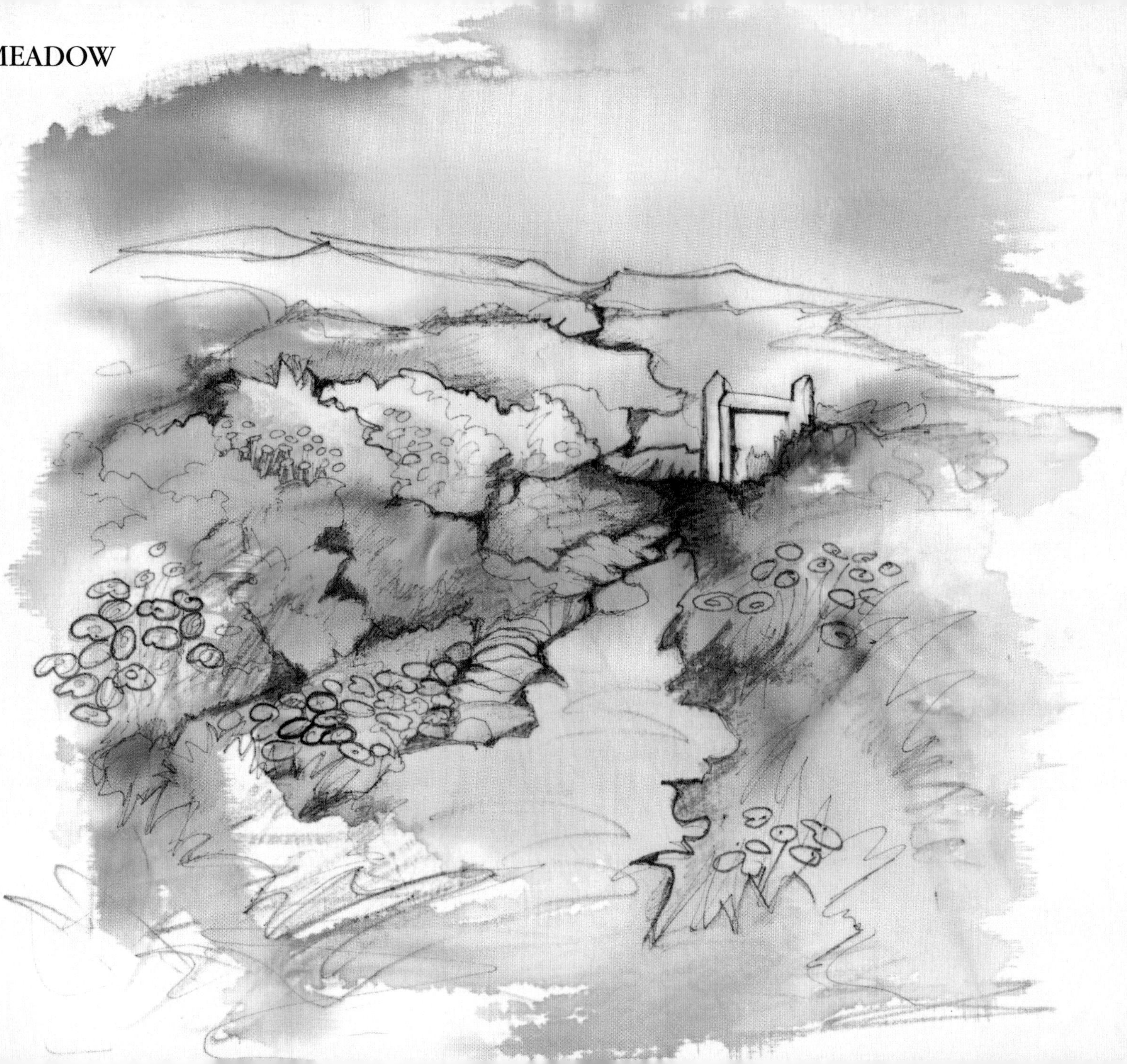

(See page 25 for embroidery.
A complete "how to" is on
pages 70 and 71).

FROM DAVID WITH LOVE

(See page 15 for an embroidered version.)

HAT

Buttonhole, yellow perlé no. 8

DUFFLE COAT

FILLER AND
OUTLINE: Chain, light and dark blue perlé no. 8

TOGGLE: Picot, light blue perlé no. 8

HAT

Buttonhole, light and dark b[lue] perlé no. 8

DUFFLE COAT

FILLER: Chain stitch, pale green perlé n[o.]

OUTLINE: Whipped chain, apple green perlé no. 8

TOGGLE: Picot, pale green perlé no. 8 a[nd] brown bullion

SMALL TEDDY BEAR

FACE: Long and short satin stitch, ochre crewel wool

MUZZLE: Colonial knots, pinky beige crewel wool

EARS: Buttonhole, ginger crewel wool

NOSE AND
MOUTH: Satin stitch and back stitch, ginger crewel wool

EYES: Colonial knots, black silk ribbon

BODY: Split stitch, ochre and pinky beige crewel wool

PAWS: Colonial knots, ginger crewel wool

SOFA

GINGHAM EFFECT: Running stitch, pale green perlé no. 8 with colonial knots on intersections, dark green perlé no. 8

PIPING: Overcast stem, dark green perlé no. 8

BIG TEDDY BEAR

FACE: Long and short satin stitch, 3 shades of crewel wool

EARS: Long and short satin stitch, ginger crewel wool

NOSE AND
MOUTH: Satin stitch and back stitch, ginger crewel wool

EYES: Colonial knots, black silk ribbon

BODY: Split stitch, 3 shades of crewel wool

PAWS: Colonial knots, dark brown outline with fawn filler, crewel wool

BUNNIES

RS: Tufting, pale pink crewel wool and pinky beige chain stitch.

CE: Split stitch, pinky beige crewel wool

ES: Bullion, brown floss, 2 strands

SE: Satin stitch, brown floss, 2 strands

UTH: Fly stitch, brown floss, 1 strand

TLINE: Back stitch, beige floss, 2 strands

WS: Chain stitch in pinky beige crewel wool

GS: Split stitch in pinky beige crewel wool

BLOUSE

LER: Stab stitch, pink cotton ribbon

TLINE: Stem stitch, coral floss
2 strands

LLAR: Semi-detached buttonhole in
white perlé no. 8

FFS: Cast-on buttonhole, white floss,
1 strand

APRON

LER: Split stitch. white rayon ribbon
with blue cotton
ribbon straps and waistband
couched in position

TLINE: Buttonhole in light blue cotton ribbon

FOR RUPERT AND ABIGAIL

(See page 16 for an
embroidered version.)

SHIRT AND BOW TIE

Back stitch and chain, light and dark
blue perlé no. 8

DUNGAREES

Whipped chain, alternate rows of
beige and biscuit perlé no. 8

BAG

BODY: Weaving, light and dark
blue cotton ribbon

STRAP: Plait, light and dark blue
cotton ribbon

BASKET

BODY: Chain, biscuit and brown cotton ribbon

STRAP: Chain, biscuit cotton ribbon

CUSHIONS

OUTLINE: Split stitch, pale blue soft cotton ribbon overlaid with
chain in 2 strands of medium blue floss

SHADOWS: Long and short stab stitch, light blue floss, 1 strand

TRAPUNTO QUILTING: Colonial knots, ecru perlé no. 8

THE LANDSCAPE VEGETABLE PATCH

Enjoy the different silk ribbon and crewel vegetables and the free-style element of the underpainting.

MATERIALS
- Cotton background fabric
- Muslin (foundation fabric)
- Needles (crewel no. 8, straw needle for bullions and cast-on buttonhole and chenille needle for ribbon work)
- A selection of embroidery threads and ribbons

INSTRUCTIONS
Ink and paint the basic design (see Frivolous Fun, page 11). Baste (tack) the muslin behind the background fabric. Study the sketch on the opposite page and the full colour picture on page 21, the crewel stitch glossary, silk ribbon basics then choose your favourite vegetable interpretations.

All the embroidery is in two strands unless otherwise stated.

SUN FLOWER
FLOWER:	Inverted stab stitch, yellow silk ribbon.
CENTRE:	Colonial knots, dark brown floss.
LEAVES:	Stab stitch, rayon ribbon overlaid with feather stitch, green floss, single strand.

ARTICHOKE
HEAD:	Mock bullion, grey/green silk ribbon.
LEAVES:	Stab stitch, green silk ribbon.
STEMS:	Whipped chain, green floss.

BEANS
BODY:	Double-sided cast-on buttonhole, bright green floss.
STEM:	Chain stitch, green floss.
LEAVES:	Fly stitch, green cotton ribbon.
STAKE:	Overcast stem, brown floss.

LAVENDER
LEAVES:	Feather stitch, green floss.
FLOWERS:	Bullion, lilac floss.

DILL
STEM:	Back stitch, green floss.
LEAVES:	Fly stitch, green floss.
FLOWERS:	Colonial knots, yellow floss.

PUMPKIN
BODY:	Split stitch outlined in chain stitch, yellow and orange floss.
LEAVES:	Lazy daisy, colonial knot, variegated green silk ribbon.

SPRING ONIONS
FOLIAGE:	Couched, rayon ribbon.

CAULIFLOWER
HEAD:	Colonial knots, white perlé no. 8.
LEAVES:	Cast-on buttonhole, green crewel wool.

LETTUCE
HEAD:	Ruched, green silk ribbon.

MARIGOLDS
FLOWER:	Colonial knots, yellow and orange floss.
LEAVES:	Lazy daisy, green silk ribbon.

NASTURTIUMS
FLOWER:	Buttonhole pin-wheel, yellow, orange and red floss, single strand.
LEAVES:	Buttonhole pinwheel, green floss, single strand.

CHIVES
FLOWERS:	Bullion, lilac floss.
STEMS:	Whipped chain, green floss.

RHUBARB
LEAVES:	Lazy daisy, green floss.
STEMS:	Chain stitch, plum floss.

BRUSSEL SPROUTS
HEAD:	Colonial knots, burgundy and green floss.
LEAVES:	Rumanian, green and plum floss.

COMFREY
LEAVES:	Rumanian, green floss.

TOMATOES
STEM:	Overcast stem, green floss.
LEAVES:	Stab stitch, fly stitch, variegated silk ribbon.
FRUIT:	Colonial knots, shades of red floss.

CORN
EAR:	Wheat-ear stitch, golden yellow floss.
LEAVES:	Stab stitch, green silk ribbon.
COB:	Picot, green floss; colonial knots, yellow floss.
BEARD:	Tufting, brown floss.

MARROW
BODY:	Colonial knots, yellow floss.
LEAVES:	Lazy daisy, variegated silk ribbon.

TURNIP
FOLIAGE:	Bullion, green gloss.

BEETROOT
LEAVES:	Bullion, green floss.
ROOT:	Bullion, burgundy floss.

CARROTS
LEAVES:	Feather stitch, green floss.
ROOT:	Cast-on buttonhole, orange floss.

NOTE: *Wet and iron your muslin before placing the muslin (foundation fabric) behind the prepared top fabric. See that the warp and the weft of the muslin and the top cotton match* (ie. the greatest stretch is in the same direction) *and baste together.*
(The muslin gives body and a foundation for beginning and ending neatly).

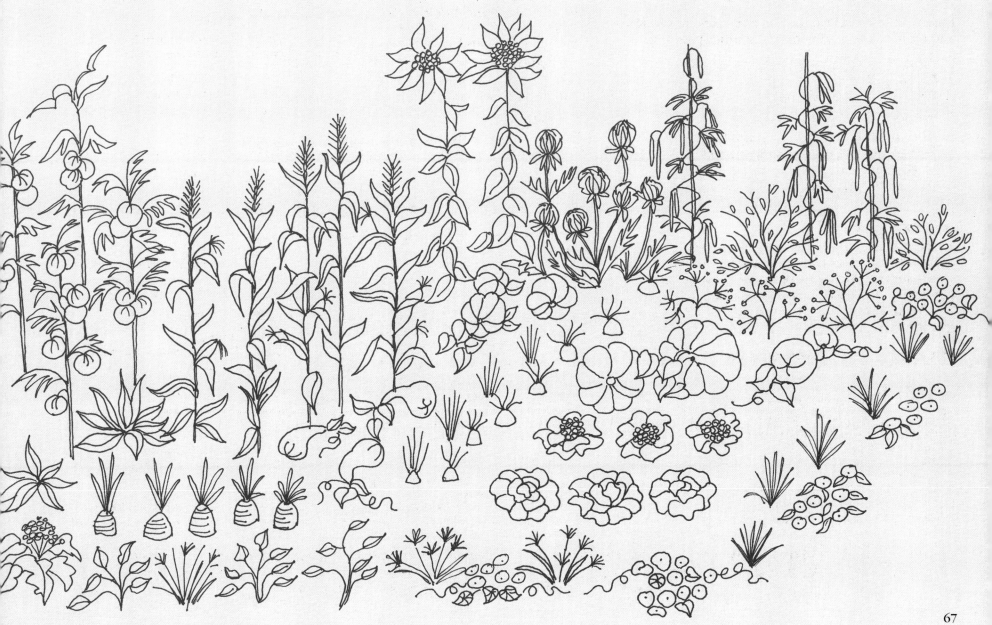

THERE IS A SEASON

Nature in all her glory is represented in this tranquil scene. Enjoy the many different crewel stitches and the free-style element of the under painting.

MATERIALS
- Cotton background fabric
- Muslin (foundation fabric)
- Needles (crewel no. 8 and a straw needle for bullions and cast-on buttonhole)
- A selection of embroidery threads

INSTRUCTIONS

Ink and paint the basic design (see Frivolous Fun, page 11). Baste (tack) the muslin behind the background fabric. Study the sketch on the opposite page, the full colour picture on page 32, and the crewel stitch glossary. Create hydrangeas, canary creepers, wisteria, ivy and forget-me-knots in one or two strands of embroidery floss. Suggest a backdrop of front door, pebbles and gardening tools with simple delineation stitches so as not to loose the charm of the underpainting.

All the embroidery is in two strands unless otherwise stated.

IVY
LEAVES:	Satin stitch on the diagonal, shades of green floss, single strand.
VEINS:	Stem stitch pale green or ecru, single strand.
STEM:	Long bullion, 1 strand each of brown and beige floss.

WISTERIA
BLOOM:	Bullion in pairs, dark and light lilac floss (2 strands of dark, one strand of light and dark, 2 strands of light floss)
STEM:	Stem stitch in green floss.

PINK HYDRANGEA
BLOOM:	Colonial knots - shades of pink and green floss (1 and 2 strands).
LEAVES:	Semi-detached buttonhole - shades of green gloss.

FORGET ME NOTS
FLOWER:	Colonial knots, 5 blue petals with yellow floss centres.
LEAVES:	Lazy daisy, dark green floss, single strand.

BASKET
Weaving, pinky beige floss.

SPADE
Chain, light grey floss, single strand.

PEBBLES
Buttonhole and colonial knots, shades of beige and grey floss.

WHITE HYDRANGEA
BLOOMS:	Colonial knots, one strand, white interspersed with pale pink and green floss.
LEAVES:	Chain in one direction, shades of green floss.
VEIN:	Whipped chain, light and dark green floss.

CANARY CREEPER
BLOOMS:	Cast-on buttonhole, light and dark yellow floss, 25 to 30 cast-on's, single strand. Extended French knots, mustard floss.
CALYX:	Bullion, green floss, single strand.

FRONT DOOR
Coral stitch, pinky brown floss, four strands.

DOOR HANDLE
Split stitch, vertical spider's web and french knots, biscuit floss with backstitch outline, pale grey floss, one strand.

STEP
Split stitch, pinky brown floss.

NOTE:
Wet and iron your muslin before placing the muslin (foundation fabric) behind the prepared top fabric. See that the warp and the weft of the muslin and the top cotton match (ie. the greatest stretch is in the same direction) *and baste together.* (The muslin gives body and a foundation for beginning and ending neatly).

CREEPY CRAWLIES

All the embroidery is in two strands unless otherwise stated.
Metallic threads are single strand.

WASP

BODY: Colonial knots and bullion, antique metallic gold.

TINY BEE (1)

WINGS: Stab stitch, pale blue organdie ribbon stabilised with antique gold thread.

BODY: Bullions, yellow and black floss.

TINY BEE (2)

WINGS: 3D loop, light blue oragandie ribbon, stabilised with charcoal floss.

BODY: Cast-on buttonhole, antique gold thread.

BUMBLE BEE

WINGS: Stab stitch, rust floss.

BODY: Bullion, buttonhole and satin stitch, yellow and gold thread.

FUZZY BEE

WINGS: Stab stitch, silver metallic thread.

BODY: Turkey work (tufting), yellow and charcoal floss.

FEELERS: Extended French knots, gold metallic thread.

ROSE-BEETLE

BODY: Stab stitch, cinnamon silk ribbon.

HEAD: Stab stitch, black floss and gold metallic thread.

FEELERS: Colonial knots, black floss.

CRAZY BEETLE

WINGS: Feather stitch, apricot floss.

BODY: Satin stitch and stab stitch, bottle green and black floss.

HEAD: Rumanian and satin stitch, apricot and black floss.

CRAZY BEETLE (Flying)

WINGS: Feather stitch, apricot and gold thread.

BODY: Satin stitch, bottle green floss.

FANTASY BEETLE

WINGS: Inverted stab stitch, pink organdie ribbon stabilised with pink floss.

BODY: Satin stitch, bottle green floss.

HEAD: Mock bullion, mustard silk ribbon.

LADYBIRD (Bold)

BODY: Rumanian or satin stitch with colonial knots, red and black floss.

HEAD: Satin stitch, black floss.

FEELERS
AND LEGS: Stab stitch, black floss.

LADYBIRD (Delicate)

BODY: Stab stitch and colonial knots, red organdie ribbon and black floss.

LILAC BUTTERFLY (Side View)

WINGS: Cast-on buttonhole, lazy daizy and fly stitch, lilac, teal blue and gold thread.

BODY: Bullion and colonial knot, lilac and black floss.

RUST BUTTERFLY (Side View)

WINGS: Cast-on buttonhole, lazy daisy and fly stitch, mustard, rust and gold thread.

DELICATE BUTTERFLY

WINGS: Buttonhole and colonial knots, apple green floss.

BODY: Bullions, dark green floss.

BOLD BUTTERFLY

WINGS: Stab stitch, bottle green organdie ribbon and pale blue organdie ribbon stabilised with stab stitch, rose pink silk ribbon and floss.

BODY: Bullions and colonial knot, mustard floss.

GREEN MOTH

WINGS: Buttonhole, satin stitch and lazy daisy, bottle green and mustard floss, and gold metallic thread.

BODY: Stab stitch, bottle green silk ribbon stabilised with feather stitch and colonial knots, bottle green floss.

PINK AND MUSTARD MOTH

WINGS: Stab stitch and lazy daisy, rose pink, mustard and white silk ribbon stabilised with stab stitch, bottle green floss.

BOLD GNAT

WINGS: Inverted stab stitch, plum organdie ribbon stabilised with stab stitch, antique gold metallic thread.

BODY: Bullions, antique gold metallic thread.

DELICATE GNAT

WINGS: Back stitch, antique gold metallic thread.

BODY: Bullion and colonial knot, dark green floss.

FLY

WINGS: Inverted stab stitch, charcoal organdie ribbon stabilised with stab stitch, charcoal floss.

FLYING INSECT

WINGS: Inverted stab stitch, bottle green organdie ribbon stabilised with feather stitch, apricot floss.

DRAGON FLY

WINGS: Inverted stab stitch, charcoal organdie ribbon stabilised with colonial knots, silver metallic thread.

BODY: Lazy daisy, satin stitch and colonial knots, teal blue floss stabilised with stab stitch, silver metallic thread.

MOSQUITO

BODY: Bullion and colonial knots, yellow and silver thread.

WINGS: Stab stitch, silver metallic thread.

ANTS

HEAD AND BODY: Colonial knot and bullions, black, charcoal or antique gold thread.

GRASSHOPPER

LEGS: Bullions, apple green floss; back stitch, black floss.

WORM

Bullions and fly stitch, light and dark green floss.

SNAIL (1)

SHELL: Colonial knot and vertical spiders web, brown floss; back stitch, black floss.

SNAIL (2)

SHELL: Woven spiders web and buttonhole, brown floss; back stitch, black floss.

FEELERS: Extended french knots, cinnamon floss.

SNAIL (3)

SHELL: Bullions, antique gold metallic thread.

BODY: Colonial knots, cinnamon floss.

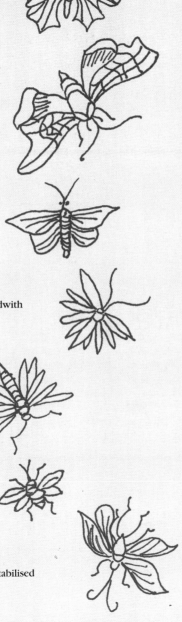

71

FRESH WATER TROUT

(See page 41 for an embroidered version in metallic threads.)

All the embroidery is in single strand unless otherwise stated.

BROWN TROUT

BODY: Green, rust and ecru organdie ribbon held in place with matching whipped chain outline and overlaid with colonial knots, antique gold metallic thread

TAIL: Stem stitch, teal, grey and green floss

GILL: Buttonhole and back stitch, metallic thread

EYE: Buttonhole pin-wheel, antique gold metallic thread

BODY OUTLINE: Whipped chain, teal and ecru floss, 2 strands

UPPER FIN: Chain stitch, mixed metallics – silver, pink and turquoise

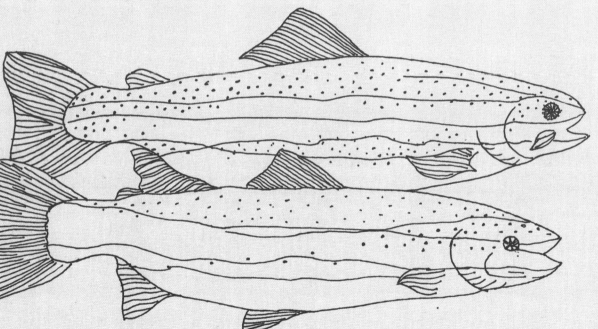

RAINBOW TROUT

BODY: Grey, apricot and ecru, organdie ribbon held in place with whipped chain in teal floss, 2 strands and overlaid with metallic colonial knots

TAIL: Split stitch, metallics and shades of grey floss (2 strands)

GILL: Buttonhole and back stitch, metallic thread

EYE: Spider's web, metallic thread with tiny bead in the centre

UPPER FIN: Long thin bullions, metallic thread and grey floss

LOWER FIN: Lazy daisy, mixed metallics

SALMON AND TROUT FLIES

(See page 49 for an embroidered picture with a frame.)

THUNDERSTOAT.

ALEXANDRA.

BLUE CHARM

LOGIE

GROUSE AND GREEN

TIPPET SILVER

THE GAZEBO

(See page 30 for an embroidered version.)

All the embroidery is in single strand unless otherwise stated.

GAZEBO
Lattice couching, white perlé no. 8 and green floss

STANDARD ROSE
FLOWER: Woven spider's web, white silk ribbon

LEAF: Stab stitch, green silk ribbon

STEM: Whipped chain, brown floss (2 strands)

TINY DAISY
FLOWER: Colonial knots, purple and
yellow silk ribbon and
purple and yellow floss

ROSE BUD BUSH
FLOWERS: Bullion, light and dark pink floss

STEMS: Coral stitch, green floss (2 strands)

LEAVES: Lazy daisy, green floss (2 strands)

LARGE LEAVES
Rumanian and fish bone, shades
of green floss (2 strands)

PAVING STONES
Colonial knots, pink and apricot floss

CREEPER
FLOWERS: Ruched petals, coffee silk ribbon

STEM: Chain stitch, light brown floss

LEAVES: Lazy daisy, avocado green silk ribbon

FOLIAGE IN POTS
LEAVES: Woven picot, dark green floss
(2 strands); rumanian, olive green
floss; fish bone, green floss; stab
stitch, green silk ribbon and
green floss

IRIS
FLOWER: Iris stitch, mustard silk ribbon
and bullion, yellow floss

STEMS: Stem stitch, green floss

3D PETAL DAISY
FLOWER: 3D Loop, shades of pink silk ribbon

CENTRE: French knots, yellow floss (2 strands)

LEAVES: Fly stitch, dark green silk ribbon

POTS
Chain stitch, khaki floss

PANSIES
FLOWER: Cast-on buttonhole, light
and dark blue floss

CENTRE: Colonial knots, yellow floss

LEAVES: Colonial knots, dark green floss

VIOLETS
FLOWERS: Stab stitch, purple silk ribbon

CENTRE: Colonial knot, yellow silk ribbon

LEAF: Buttonhole pinwheel, dark green floss

WHITE TULIPS
FLOWER: Stab stitch, white silk ribbon and fly stitch, mustard floss

STEMS: Whipped back stitch, green floss

LEAVES: Inverted stab stitch, light green silk ribbon

73

AFRICAN BUTTERFLIES

All the embroidery is in single strand
unless otherwise stated.

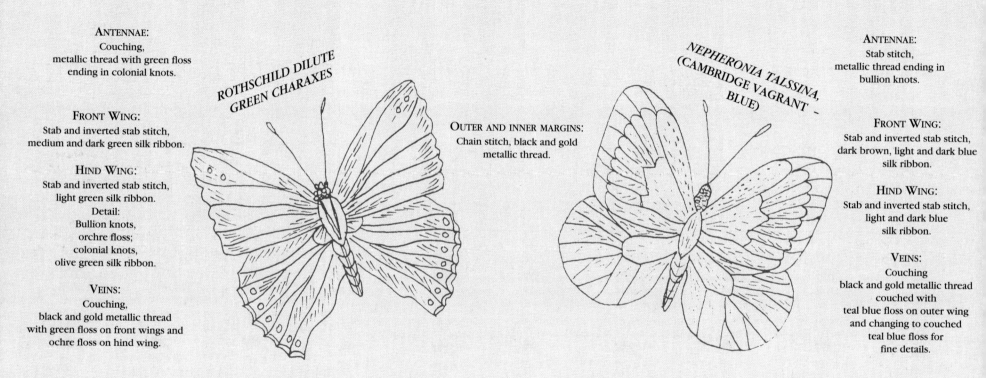

ANTENNAE:
Couching,
metallic thread with green floss
ending in colonial knots.

FRONT WING:
Stab and inverted stab stitch,
medium and dark green silk ribbon.

HIND WING:
Stab and inverted stab stitch,
light green silk ribbon.
Detail:
Bullion knots,
ochre floss;
colonial knots,
olive green silk ribbon.

VEINS:
Couching,
black and gold metallic thread
with green floss on front wings and
ochre floss on hind wing.

SHADING:
Long and short stab stitch,
matching floss,
light, medium and dark green floss.

ROTHSCHILD DILUTE GREEN CHARAXES

OUTER AND INNER MARGINS:
Chain stitch, black and gold
metallic thread.

BODY:
Colonial knots, stab stitch and fly stitch,
olive green silk ribbon.
Fine detail:
Colonial knots, stab stitch and fly stitch,
metallic thread.

*NEPHERONIA TALSSINA,
(CAMBRIDGE VAGRANT –
BLUE)*

ANTENNAE:
Stab stitch,
metallic thread ending in
bullion knots.

FRONT WING:
Stab and inverted stab stitch,
dark brown, light and dark blue
silk ribbon.

HIND WING:
Stab and inverted stab stitch,
light and dark blue
silk ribbon.

VEINS:
Couching
black and gold metallic thread
couched with
teal blue floss on outer wing
and changing to couched
teal blue floss for
fine details.

BODY:
Stab stitch and fly stitch,
chocolate brown silk ribbon.
Fine detail:
Colonial knots, stab stitch and fly stitch,
matching brown floss.

SHADING:
Long and short stab stitch
white and blue floss.

AFRICAN BUTTERFLIES

All the embroidery is in single strand
unless otherwise stated.

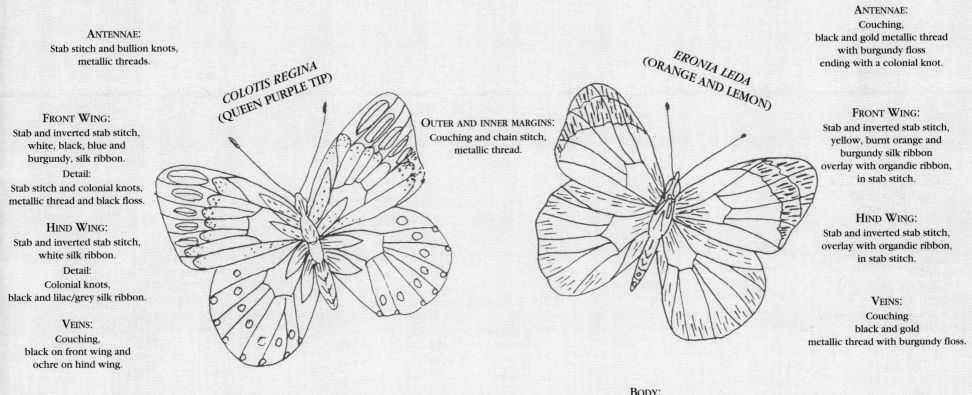

COLOTIS REGINA (QUEEN PURPLE TIP)

ERONIA LEDA (ORANGE AND LEMON)

ANTENNAE:
Stab stitch and bullion knots,
metallic threads.

FRONT WING:
Stab and inverted stab stitch,
white, black, blue and
burgundy, silk ribbon.
Detail:
Stab stitch and colonial knots,
metallic thread and black floss.

HIND WING:
Stab and inverted stab stitch,
white silk ribbon.
Detail:
Colonial knots,
black and lilac/grey silk ribbon.

VEINS:
Couching,
black on front wing and
ochre on hind wing.

OUTER AND INNER MARGINS:
Couching and chain stitch,
metallic thread.

SHADING:
Stab stitch
beige and misty blue organdie ribbon.
Detail:
Stab stitch
charcoal floss.

BODY:
Stab stitch
burgundy silk ribbon
Stab stitch, fly stitch and colonial knots
charcoal floss.

ANTENNAE:
Couching,
black and gold metallic thread
with burgundy floss
ending with a colonial knot.

FRONT WING:
Stab and inverted stab stitch,
yellow, burnt orange and
burgundy silk ribbon
overlay with organdie ribbon,
in stab stitch.

HIND WING:
Stab and inverted stab stitch,
overlay with organdie ribbon,
in stab stitch.

VEINS:
Couching
black and gold
metallic thread with burgundy floss.

BODY:
Mock bullion, stab stitch and colonial knots,
burgundy silk ribbon
Detail:
Colonial knots and bullion knots,
bottle green floss.

SHADING:
Long and short stab stitch,
matching floss,
yellow, orange and burgundy.

ROCKING CHAIR

All the embroidery is in single strand unless otherwise stated.

See Introduction page for a small colour picture.

BIRD'S CAGE

Chain stitch, metallic thread

HYDRANGEA

FLOWER: Colonial knot, blue and plum silk ribbon

LEAVES: Inverted stab stitch, green silk ribbon

Select any of the following stitches for the flower pots

STITCHES OF POTS

1) Chain stitch
2) French knot
3) Satin stitch
4) Buttonhole
5) Lattic couching
} Apricot floss, green terracotta or light and dark brown floss

CENTRE TABLE

LILY LEAF: Buttonhole pinwheel, dark green floss

PANSY: Cast-on buttonhole, light and dark blue floss
Leaves: Lazy daisy, dark green floss

IVY LEAVES: Satin stitch and back stitch, dark green floss

NASTURTIUM: Stab stitch and mock bullion, red and yellow silk ribbon
Leaves: Buttonhole pinwheel, dark green floss

VIOLETS: Lazy daisy, purple floss

DEW DROPS: Colonial knot, coffee silk ribbon
Leaves: Fly stitch, green floss

BUTTERCUP: Inverted stab stitch, yellow silk ribbon
Stems: Stem stitch and bullion, light green floss

BACKGROUND FOLIAGE: Rumanian, green floss

3D PETAL DAISY CREEPER

FLOWER: 3D loop, cherry silk ribbon

CENTRE: Colonial knot, yellow floss

LEAVES: Lazy daisy, dark green silk ribbon

LARGE RED DAISY

FLOWER: Inverted stab stitch, deep red silk ribbon

CENTRE: Colonial knot, yellow floss

LEAVES: Rumanian, green floss

ROSE CREEPER

FLOWER: Spider's web rose, shades of pink silk ribbon

BUDS: Colonial knot and lazy daisy, shades of pink silk ribbon

LEAVES: Inverted stab stitch, shades of green silk ribbon

CANOPY

Cast-on buttonhole, brown floss

WINDOW

OUTLINE: Chain stitch, brown flo

LILY CREEPE

FLOWER: Stab stitch, white silk ribbon

CENTRE: Bullion, yello floss

LEAVES: Woven picot, dark green flos (2 strands)

ROCKING CHAI

OUTLINE: Chain stitch, dark green floss

CUSHIONS: Lattice couchi light and dark pink floss (2 strands)

IRIS

FLOWER: Iris stitch, light an dark purple silk ribbon

CENTRE: Bullion, yellow flos

STEMS: Stem stitch, green flo

LEAVES: Inverted stab stitch, green silk ribbon

FUCHSIA

FLOWER: Inverted stab stitch, shades of pink silk ribbon

STAMENS: Extended french knot, yellow floss

STEMS: Stem stitch, olive green floss

LEAVES: Inverted stab stitch, green silk ribbon

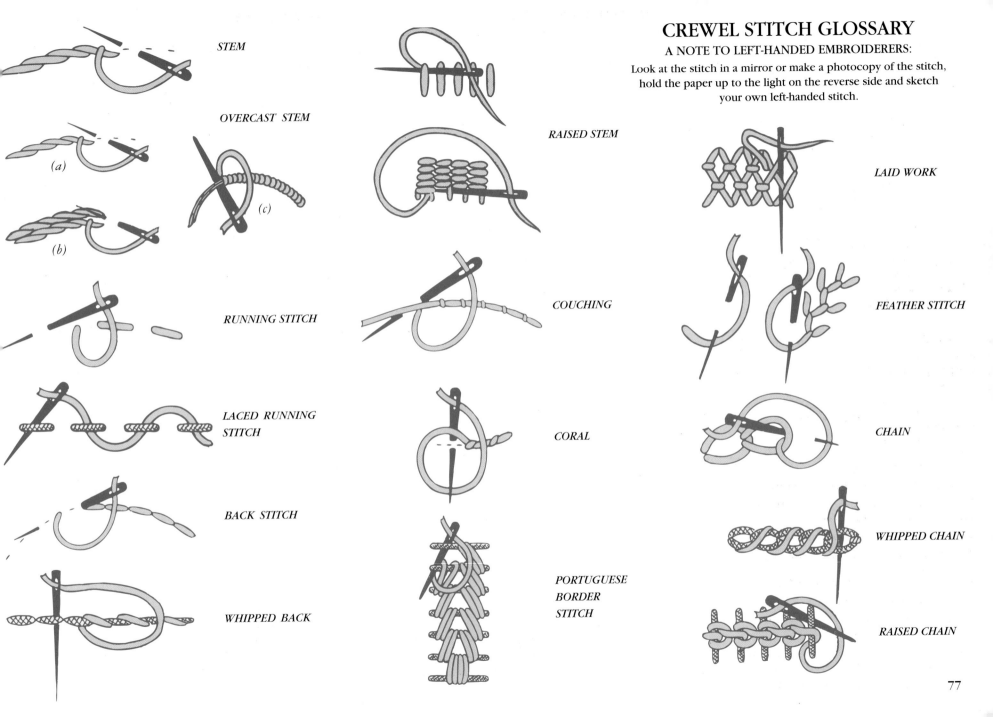

CREWEL STITCH GLOSSARY

A NOTE TO LEFT-HANDED EMBROIDERERS:

Look at the stitch in a mirror or make a photocopy of the stitch, hold the paper up to the light on the reverse side and sketch your own left-handed stitch.

STEM

OVERCAST STEM

(a)

(b)

(c)

RAISED STEM

LAID WORK

RUNNING STITCH

COUCHING

FEATHER STITCH

LACED RUNNING STITCH

CORAL

CHAIN

BACK STITCH

WHIPPED CHAIN

WHIPPED BACK

PORTUGUESE BORDER STITCH

RAISED CHAIN

77

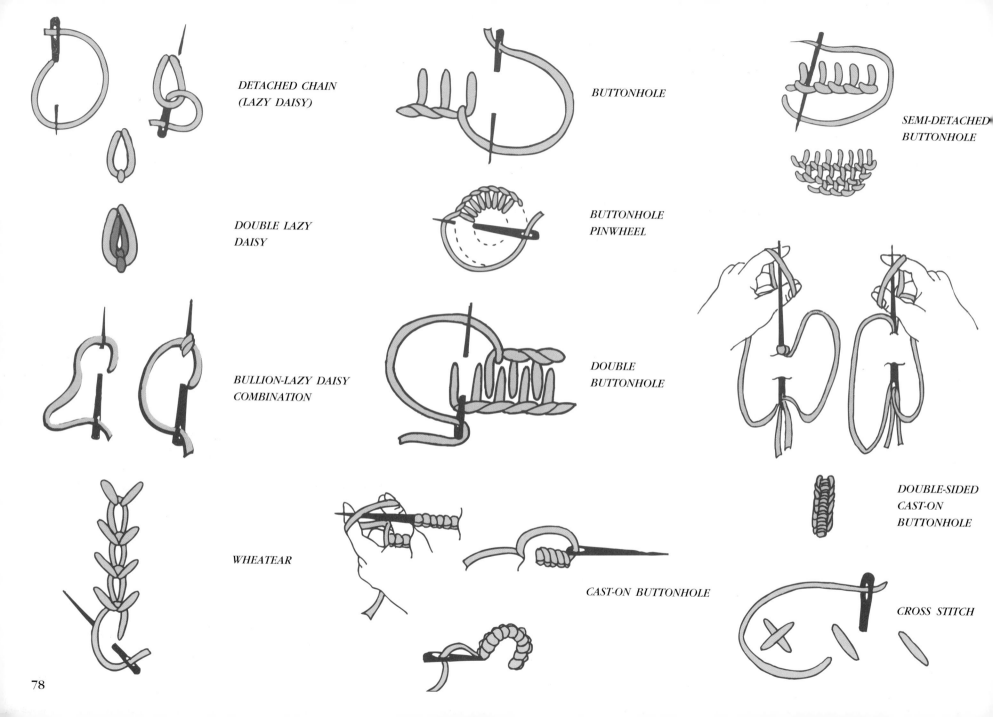

DETACHED CHAIN
(LAZY DAISY)

BUTTONHOLE

SEMI-DETACHED
BUTTONHOLE

DOUBLE LAZY
DAISY

BUTTONHOLE
PINWHEEL

BULLION-LAZY DAISY
COMBINATION

DOUBLE
BUTTONHOLE

DOUBLE-SIDED
CAST-ON
BUTTONHOLE

WHEATEAR

CAST-ON BUTTONHOLE

CROSS STITCH

78

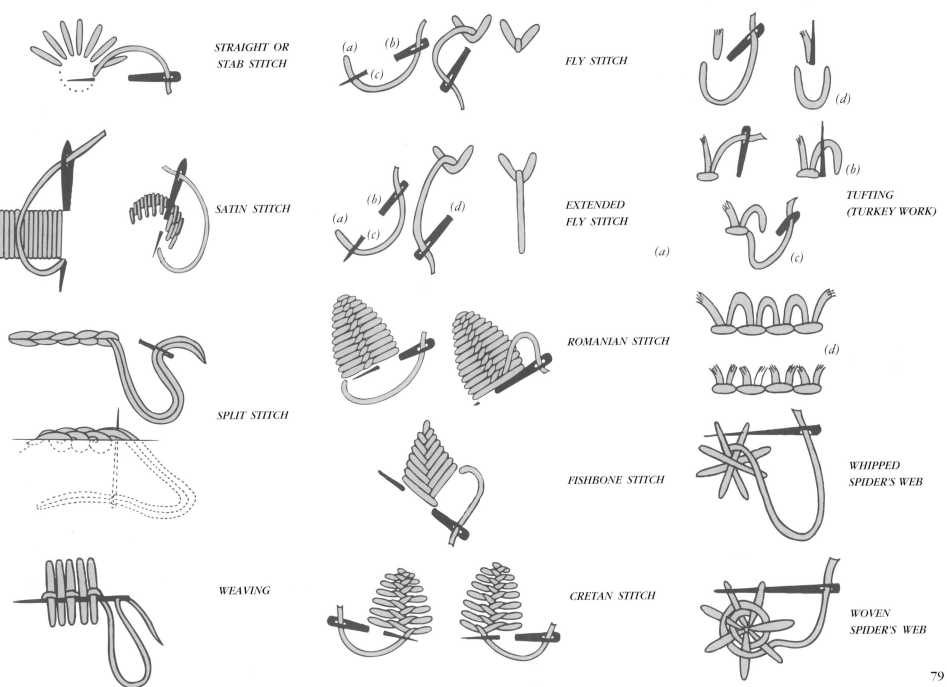

STRAIGHT OR
STAB STITCH

FLY STITCH

(a)

(b)

(c)

(d)

SATIN STITCH

EXTENDED
FLY STITCH

(a)

(b)

(c)

(d)

TUFTING
(TURKEY WORK)

(a)

(b)

(c)

(d)

SPLIT STITCH

ROMANIAN STITCH

FISHBONE STITCH

WHIPPED
SPIDER'S WEB

WEAVING

CRETAN STITCH

WOVEN
SPIDER'S WEB

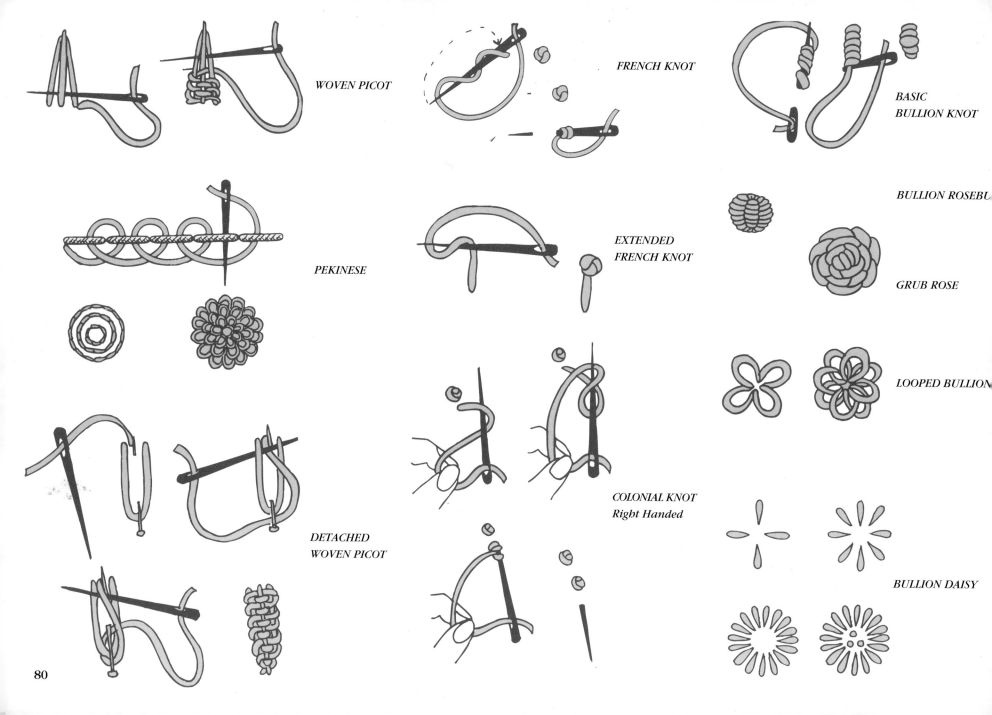

WOVEN PICOT

FRENCH KNOT

BASIC
BULLION KNOT

PEKINESE

EXTENDED
FRENCH KNOT

BULLION ROSEBU

GRUB ROSE

LOOPED BULLION

DETACHED
WOVEN PICOT

COLONIAL KNOT
Right Handed

BULLION DAISY

80